MW01296143

Enjoying the Book of Ruth:
The Bible in Rhyme

Marcia Goldlist

Property of
BETH MEYER CONGREGATION

Primary Bible

22-112

Copyright © 2015 Marcia Goldlist

All rights reserved.

ISBN-10: 1511848391
ISBN-13: 978-1511848398

All rights reserved. You may freely recite any part of this book for classes or sermons but no part of this publication may be reproduced for profit, or transmitted by any means – electronic, mechanical, photographic (photocopying), recording, or otherwise – without prior permission in writing from the author. If you think that someone else would like this book please ask them to buy it. Please do not photocopy this book for class, or group purposes. Every student should purchase his/her own book. Please respect the time and creative energy of the author.

Also by Marcia Goldlist

The Bible in Rhyme Series

Enjoying Genesis
Enjoying Genesis in Large Print
Enjoying Genesis: The Bible in Rhyme Workbook
Enjoying Exodus
Enjoying the Book of Esther

Express Yourself in Rhyme Series

Birthday Cards & Toasts
Cards & Toasts for Almost All Occasions
Cards, Toasts & Notes for the Office
The Big Book of Cards & Toasts for Almost All Occasions

Blog Site

enjoyingthebible.wordpress.com

Marcia's Author Page

http://www.amazon.com/author/marciagoldlist

TABLE OF CONTENTS

Acknowledgement

Special thanks once again to Raanan Eichler, researcher and occasional lecturer of Bible.

CHAPTER ONE

In the days when the judges' were in command,

There was a famine in the land.

From Bethlehem in Judah, a man, his wife, and his two

sons went away.

To the fields of Moab they went to stay.

His name was Elimelech, and Naomi was his wife;

Mahlon and Kilion were their sons whom they brought to

life.

They were Ephratites from Bethlehem in Judah, and they

came

To the fields of Moab with an aim.

Once they got there, they did not stray.

There they did stay.

Elimelech, the husband of Naomi died.

She was left with her two sons by her side.

After he was buried,

Moabite women the sons both married.

Orpah, was the name of one,

And Ruth was married to the other son.

For about ten years duration

They lived in that location.

Then Mahlon and Kilion also died,

And the woman was left without her two sons and her
husband by her side.

She, and her daughters-in-law, got up from the fields of
Moab to return,

Because in the fields of Moab she did learn

That God remembered His nation

And was once again allowing bread creation.

From the place where she had been she went away.

Her two daughters-in-law went with her on her way.

They set out on the roadway

To return to the land of Judah without delay.

Then to her two daughters-in-law Naomi did say,

"Go, each of you return to your mother's house today.

May God deal kindly with you

As you have dealt kindly with the dead and with me too!

May God grant that you find rest;

Each in the home of another husband may you be blessed."

Then she gave them each a kiss.

They raised their voices and cried as her they did not want to dismiss.

To her they did say,

"With you, we will return to your people today."

To them, Naomi did say,

"My daughters, turn away.

Why should you come with me?

Are there any more sons in my womb that could be your
husbands, if you agree?

Turn back, my daughters, go on your way!

I am too old to have a husband; I will not lead you astray.

Even if I were to say that there was hope for me,

And even if tonight of a husband I had a guarantee,

And even if I had two sons by fate,

Until they grew up would you wait?

Unmarried would you remain?

From getting married to someone else would you refrain?

My daughters, no!

I am very sad for you, though,

That the hand of God did decree

To be against me."

They lifted up their voices to the sky

And again they did cry.

Orpah gave her mother-in-law a kiss.

But, her mother-in-law, Ruth would not dismiss.

So, Naomi did say,

"Look, your sister-in-law has gone away.

With me she did not stay.

She went back to her people and her gods to pray.

With her return.

Do not let me be of concern."

But Ruth replied,

"Do not urge me to leave your side,

Or to return

And not follow you with any concern.

For wherever you go, I will go your way,

And wherever you lodge, I will also stay.

Your people will be my people, and your God my God

on high.

Where you die, I will die.

And to be buried there I agree.

All this may God do to me,

And more too,

If anything but death separates me from you."

When to Naomi it was clear

That about coming with her Ruth was sincere,

About these things she no longer talked,

And the two of them until Bethlehem walked.

When they arrived in Bethlehem and they were sighted,

The entire town was excited.

And the women did say,

"Could this be Naomi whom we see today?"

"Do not call me Naomi," was her plea.

"Call me Mara, as God has dealt bitterly with me.

I was full when I went away,

But God brought me back empty today.

To be called Naomi, I do not agree,

As God has testified against me.

Misfortune I could not flee:

God has brought it upon me."

So, Naomi returned to her land

With Ruth, the Moabite, her daughter-in-law, hand-in-hand.

From the fields of Moab she returned with reason

To Bethlehem, at the beginning of the barley harvest season.

CHAPTER TWO

Naomi had a relative on her husband's side;

A mighty man of wealth who had much to provide.

From the family of Elimelech he came.

Boaz was his name.

Ruth the Moabitess, to Naomi said,

"To the field let me head,

And I will glean among the ears of grain,

Behind someone whose favor I will gain."

"My daughter, go ahead,"

She said.

So to the field she went,

And she began to glean behind the harvesters as was her intent.

It was fate that for her plan

She picked the field of Boaz, who was from Elimelech's
clan.

Boaz arrived from Bethlehem that day.

He greeted the harvesters without delay.

"God be with you!" he did say.

"May God bless you," they responded right away.

Then Boaz asked his servant

Whose job it was over the harvesters to be observant,

"To whom does this young woman belong?"

"She is a Moabite girl who with Naomi came along;

From the fields of Moab she came,"

The servant who was overseeing the harvesters did claim.

"'Please let me glean and gather,' she did ask,

'Among the sheaves after the harvesters as is my task.'

She has been on her feet from then until now,

Except for a short rest in the shelter which she did
allow."

Boaz to Ruth made a plea:

"My daughter, listen to me!

Do not go to glean in another field

For your yield.

From here don't go away;

Close to my maidens stay.

Your eyes you should keep

On the field which they reap.

Behind them walk.

To the young men I did talk

And told them not to pursue

Or molest you.

And when you are thirsty know

That to the jugs that the men have filled, you may go."

She fell on her face,

Bowing down to the ground in her place.

She asked him, "To what is it due

That I found favor with you?

Why do you take special note of me

Even though a foreigner, you know me to be?"

To her Boaz did say,

"I have been well informed of the way

That after your husband did die

Your mother-in-law you stood by.

For her you did care.

And I am aware

That to her you did cleave,

That your father and your mother you did leave.

In your land you did not stay.

You went away.

You took a stand

And left your land.

And to a people that you did not know

You did go.

May God repay you

For all that you did do.

From the Lord,

The God of Israel, a full reward

May you discover,

As under His wings you have come to take cover."

She said, "My lord, may I continue to

Please you

Because you have comforted me from the start

And spoken to your handmaid's heart,

Notwithstanding

That I do not have your handmaid's standing."

When it was time to eat,

Boaz told her to come over and have a seat.

To her he said,

"Come over and eat some of the bread.

Take a bit

And in vinegar dip it."

So beside the harvesters she sat in his domain,

And by the harvesters she was handed parched grain.

She ate

And was satisfied and had some left on her plate.

Then she got up to glean in the field,

And to his young men, Boaz appealed,

"Grain from the sheaves let her claim.

Do not put her to shame.

And even pull some grain

From the bundles on purpose for her to claim.

And you are not

To rebuke her for what she got."

So, she gleaned what she could claim

Until evening came.

She then beat out what she had gleaned from the estate,

And it came to about an ephah of barley by weight.

She took all that she had earned,

And to the town she returned.

All that she did glean

By her mother-in-law was seen.

Ruth also took out and gave

Her left-over food which she did save.

Her mother-in-law to her did say,

"Where did you glean today?"

"And where did you work," she asked too.

And she added, "Bless the one that took notice of you."

To her mother-in-law she did say,

"I worked by a man named Boaz today."

To her daughter-in-law, Naomi did say,

"May he be blessed by God, I pray.

For he did not shed

His kindness to the living or the dead."

To her Naomi also stated,

"To us he is related.

He is a close relation,

So he has a redeemer's designation."

Ruth the Moabite did say,

"He even told me close to his workers to stay

On his domain

Until cut is all the grain."

Naomi, to her daughter-in-law, Ruth, did say,

"It is good that with his young women you stay,

As it is true

That on another field someone may harass you."

So, close to Boaz's young women she did stay:

Until the end of the barley harvest and the wheat harvest
she did not stray.

And she did reside

With her mother-in-law side-by-side.

CHAPTER THREE

To Ruth, Naomi, her mother-in-law, did say,

"My daughter, I will find you a place to stay

Where you can find rest

And you will be blessed.

Now, Boaz, our relation,

With whose young women you have worked on location,

Will tonight be doing his chore

Of winnowing barley on the threshing floor.

So get clean from your soil

And anoint yourself with oil.

Get dressed in your finest clothes

And go down to the threshing floor, I propose.

But, until he has finished drinking and eating,

Do not make yourself known through any greeting.

When he lies down to sleep,

The place in your mind keep.

Go over and take off the cover from his feet so that they are bare

And lie down there.

Then he will tell you

What you are to do."

Ruth did say,

"Everything that you have told me to do, I will do today."

So, she went down to the threshing floor

And did everything that her mother-in-law instructed her before.

When Boaz finished eating and drinking, his heart was merry.

To lie down at the end of the grain pile he did not tarry.

She came softly and uncovered his feet so that they were

bare,

And she lied down there.

In the middle of the night,

The man had a little fright.

He turned,

And that a woman was lying at his feet, he learned.

"Who are you?" he asked in dismay.

"I am Ruth, your handmaid," she did say.

"That you spread your cover over your handmaid is my

plea,

As you are a redeemer to me."

"Be blessed by God, my daughter," he did say,

"As your latest display

Of kindness is even greater than your first;

As for the younger men you did not thirst:

Not for the poor ones,

Nor the rich sons.

And now, my daughter, do not fear,

For to whatever you ask, I will adhere.

To all the people living within the gates of my town it is
known

That yourself to be a virtuous woman you have shown.

Now, while it is true that I am a redeeming relation,

There is a relative of a closer station.

Stay the night.

Then, in the morning, if he redeems you from your
plight,

That will be fine.

But if to redeem you he does decline,

Then the redemption I will give,

God does live!

Now lie down until

The morning and be still."

So she lay down by his feet until the morning,

And she woke before one could recognize another,
because he gave this warning:

"Let it not be known

That the woman came to the threshing floor alone."

To her he did declare,

"Bring the shawl that you wear.

Hold it out

And grasp it about."

She held her shawl like a board,

And into it six measures of barley he poured.

He laid it on her, her food to augment,

And to the town he went.

She came to her mother-in-law who to her did say,

"My daughter, how do things stand with you today?"

So Ruth told

Her all that with the man did unfold.

And she did explain,

"These six measures of barley I did obtain,

As to me

He did decree,

'Do not go back and stand

Before your mother-in-law with an empty hand.'"

Then she did say,

"Sit still, my daughter, do not move away

Until you know

How the matter did go.

To rest, the man will not give way

Until he has finished the matter today."

CHAPTER FOUR

Meanwhile, Boaz went up to the gate

And sat, until, by fate,

The redeeming relation that Boaz did mention

Walked by and got his attention.

"Come over here, so-and-so, and sit down," Boaz did
say.

So he came over and sat down for a short stay.

He then took ten

Of the town's elder men.

He said, "Sit down here with us."

So they sat down without a fuss.

Then he made to the redeeming relation

The following declaration:

"Naomi, I have learned

From the field of Moab has returned.

And the parcel of land is to be sold

Which our brother, Elimelech, did hold.

And since I knew,

I thought that I should tell you.

Before those that sit at hand

And before the elders of my people, buy the land.

If to redeem it you agree,

So it will be.

But if your answer is 'no'

And it is not to be redeemed, I want to know,

Because there is no one to redeem it other than you,

And I am after you in the queue."

Then the redeemer did say,

"To redeem it, I am willing to pay."

Then Boaz did say,

"On the day

That you buy the field of land

From Naomi's hand,

Ruth the Moabite you must also buy,

As she is the wife of the son that did die,

And you must raise up the name of the deceased first
hand

To inherit the land.

The redeeming relation did reply,

"Then I cannot comply,

As it might endanger the fate

Of my own estate.

You take the responsibility from me,

As to do it, I do not agree."

In the past

This is what was asked

In Israel concerning all things that were redeemed and
exchanged

To confirm all things that were arranged:

A man would take off his shoe,

And to give it to his friend he would follow through.

This was the action

Taken to legalize a transaction.

So, the redeeming relation to Boaz did say,

"Buy it for yourself – it is okay."

And he took off his shoe

For all to view.

Then to the elders and all the people Boaz did say,

"You are witnesses this day

That I have bought everything that was under

Elimelech's, Kilion's and Mahlon's command

From Naomi's hand.

Moreover, for my life,

Ruth the Moabitess, Mahlon's wife

I did acquire,

To be my wife as the buyer,

In order to raise up in the name of the dead firsthand

An heir for his land

With the aim

That his name

Will not be cut off from his family's base

And from the gate of his place.

Witnesses of this display

Are all of you today."

All the people that were at the gate did obey,

And with the elders, "We are witnesses," they did say,

"May God make this woman who is coming as a spouse

Into your house

Like Rachel and Leah who were great

As both helped to build the house of Israel into an

impressive state.

In Efrat may your worthy deeds be shown,

And in Bethlehem may your good name be known.

May the success of your house ensue

With the seed that God will give to you,

The seed of new life

From this young wife.

Like Perez's, may your house be

Whom Tamar bore unto Judah by God's decree."

So Boaz took Ruth to be part of his life,

And she became his wife.

God let her conceive,

And a son they did receive.

To Naomi, the women did say,

"Blessed be God who has not left you this day

Without a redeeming relation.

And let his name be famous in the Israelite nation.

May he be a restorer of life at this stage

And a nourisher in your old age.

That your daughter-in-law loves you

Is true.

To you, more than seven sons is her worth,

And she is the one, to him, that gave birth."

Naomi took the boy

And laid him in her bosom with joy.

And she did immerse

Herself in becoming his nurse.

The women who were her neighbors gave him a name.

"There is a son born to Naomi," they did proclaim.

Obed, they called his name,

The father of Jesse, the father of David; he is the same.

From Perez these are the generations

Of his relations:

Perez had Hezron, who had Ram, who had Amminadav,
who had Nahshon, who had Salma as his son;

Salma had Boaz, who had Obed, who had Jesse, who had
David as his loved one.

ABOUT THE AUTHOR

Marcia Goldlist was born in Toronto, Canada. She has a Masters of Education from the University of Toronto and a Bachelor of Education in religious education from McGill University.

Marcia loves being a grandmother and a mother.

Also by Marcia Goldlist

The Bible in Rhyme Series

Enjoying Genesis
Enjoying Genesis in Large Print
Enjoying Genesis: The Bible in Rhyme Workbook
Enjoying Exodus
Enjoying the Book of Esther

Express Yourself in Rhyme Series

Birthday Cards & Toasts
Cards & Toasts for Almost All Occasions
Cards, Toasts & Notes for the Office
The Big Book of Cards & Toasts for Almost All Occasions

Visit Marcia's Author Page:
http://www.amazon.com/author/marciagoldlist

Blog Site

enjoyingthebible.wordpress.com

Made in the USA
Columbia, SC
06 December 2022

72850617R00029